TaylorSwift

COUNTRY MUSIC'S
American Sweetheart

Mason Crest

Contents

4

6

14

58

Introduction	4
Beginnings	6
Teenage Tales	14
Girl, Interrupted	22
Global Ambition	28
Acting Her Age	36
Fact File	44
Friends and Lovers	46
Quotes	52
Discography	54
Awards and Nominations	58
Marketing the Magic	62

28

Mason Crest
450 Parkway Drive, Suite D
Broomall, PA 19008
www.masoncrest.com

Printed and bound in the United States of America.

10 9 8 7 6 5 4 3

Cataloging-in-Publication Data on file with the Library of Congress.

ISBN: 978-1-4222-3250-7
ebook ISBN: 978-1-4222-8663-0

Written by: Michael Heatley, Mike Gent and Drew Heatley

Images courtesy of PA Photos

Introduction

The girl who burst onto the scene in 2006 with her self-titled first long-player is sitting pretty at the top of the pop tree with four albums, several hit singles, and countless music-industry awards to her name. Yet she has virtually no entourage, still hangs out with childhood friends, and is someone who could easily be walked past in the street.

Taylor enjoys the best of both worlds and, unspoiled by fame, is happy enough living an everyday life off stage before lighting up the lives of her millions of fans with her music.

Swift's fourth album "Red" topped the *Billboard* 200, the UK chart, and the country albums listings in October 2012 thanks to an impressive first-week performance that gave her the third biggest-selling album of the year behind Adele's "21" and One Direction's "Up All Night." Yet her appeal is neither Ms. Adkins' big voice or the British boy band's sex appeal but a folksy, homespun charm, and a willingness to share her innermost thoughts and secrets with her audience.

Taylor Swift's wealth was estimated in 2012 as over $165 million, and she has already started using her money and fame to support arts education, literacy, and children's charities. In short, she is a girl with a talent she has worked hard at perfecting, and this has now put her in a position to give back to the less fortunate citizens of a nation that has taken her very much to heart. Long may she sing!

Beginnings

Reading, a city of some 88,000 souls, lies in the southeast of Pennsylvania and is the seat of Berks County. It is also now famous as the birthplace of Taylor Alison Swift. Her father Scott was an alumnus of the University of Delaware where he graduated in business in 1974. He went on to become head of the Swift Group, a financial advisory service under the umbrella of Merrill Lynch, the wealth management division of the Bank of America.

On February 20, 1988 he married Andrea Gardner Finlay. Andrea also worked in finance, as a mutual fund marketing executive, but opted out of her career to give birth to Taylor on December 13, 1989. Music ran in the family, since Andrea's mother was an opera singer. "I can remember her singing, the thrill of it," Taylor said of her grandmother. "She was one of

my first inspirations."

Scott Swift bought a Christmas tree farm from a client in Montgomery County, 37 miles from Reading, and Taylor spent the early years of her life in this idyllic rural setting. Her first love was horses; the family owned several, and she competed in shows at a young age. Scott recalls that his daughter first showed musical ability as an infant. "She was always singing when she was three, five, six, seven years old. It's Taylor doing what she likes to do." Taylor herself has similar memories. "My parents have videos of me on the beach at, like, three, going up to people and singing *Lion King* songs for them. I was literally going from towel to towel, saying, 'Hi, I'm Taylor. I'm going to sing "I Just Can't Wait To Be King" for you now.'"

On March 11, 1992, Taylor was joined by a younger brother, Austin, who has often appeared, along with his friends, in Taylor's videos. Austin, who bears a striking resemblance to his sister, studied at the University of Notre Dame in Indiana and Vanderbilt University in Nashville. "He goes to college and just lives a completely different life than me," says Taylor. Austin is also a talented freelance photographer; his pictures of his sister have appeared in *People* and *Rolling Stone*.

Taylor recollects her homespun upbringing with fondness. "Growing up in Pennsylvania was awesome. I wouldn't change one thing about my childhood. We had horses and a million cats, and my brother had a huge dirt pile that we played in. Those are the memories I have of growing up in Pennsylvania – having a lot of room to run, wide open spaces."

Summers were spent at her parents' holiday home in Stone Harbor, "a cute little town" on the Jersey shore. "We lived on this basin where all this magical stuff would happen. One time a dolphin swam into our basin. We had this family of otters that would live on our dock at night. We'd turn the light on and you'd see them, you know, hanging out, just being otters. And then

■ **ABOVE:** **Taylor pictured with her mother, Andrea, at the Country Music Awards.**

one summer, there was a shark that washed up on our dock. I ended up writing a novel that summer because I wouldn't go in the water. I locked myself in the den and wrote a book. When I was fourteen. Because of a shark!"

Taylor's schooling began at the elementary Wyndcroft School in Pottstown, Pennsylvania, a private school recognized nationally for its educational excellence. She found the teachers there inspirational. At Wyndcroft, Taylor first displayed a talent for writing. Asked to write a two-sentence summary, she completed a full two-page essay.

Yet even with these clearly visible creative talents, she assumed that she would follow her parents into the financial sector. "I didn't know what a stockbroker was when I was eight, but I would just tell everybody that's what I was going to be. We'd be at, like, the first day of school and they're, like, 'So what do you guys want to be when you grow up?' And everybody's, like, 'I want to be an astronaut!' Or, like, 'I want to be a ballerina!' And I'm, like, 'I'm gonna be a financial adviser!'"

A major upheaval occurred when Taylor was in fourth grade and her family moved to Wyomissing, an affluent borough situated to the west of Reading. The nine-year-old attended the town's public schools, West Reading Elementary School and Wyomissing Area Junior/ Senior High School, and found it difficult at first in the new town. "I didn't have friends. No one talked to me. I used to go to the Wyndcroft School… and when I moved to Wyomissing I didn't know anybody."

She later spoke humorously

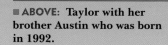
■ ABOVE: Taylor with her brother Austin who was born in 1992.

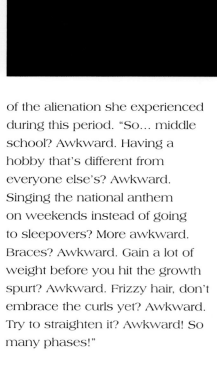

of the alienation she experienced during this period. "So… middle school? Awkward. Having a hobby that's different from everyone else's? Awkward. Singing the national anthem on weekends instead of going to sleepovers? More awkward. Braces? Awkward. Gain a lot of weight before you hit the growth spurt? Awkward. Frizzy hair, don't embrace the curls yet? Awkward. Try to straighten it? Awkward! So many phases!"

Shortly after moving to Wyomissing, Taylor began to develop an interest in musical theater and appeared in Berks Youth Theater Academy productions. "I played Sandy in *Grease*. I was an orphan in *Annie* and did *Bye-Bye Birdie* and *The Sound Of Music*." She regularly made the 130-mile journey to New York to take singing and acting lessons, but auditions in the Big Apple proved a dispiriting experience. Soon another passion took a grip on her. "I started to realize that what I looked forward to the most was the after-parties, where they had a karaoke machine set up and I could sing country music."

At age 10, Taylor was learning to sing like Faith Hill, the Dixie Chicks, and Shania Twain, Nineties "crossover country" acts that had ignited her love for the genre. Taylor began to sing wherever and whenever she could – at Boy Scout meetings, garden clubs, local festivals, or hospitals. Her father took her to the Pat Garrett Roadshow, a talent contest in nearby Strausstown, where his 11-year-old daughter won a support slot at an upcoming local Charlie Daniels gig.

After watching a VH1 television documentary on Faith Hill, Taylor realized that Nashville was the place to make her dreams reality – and, with the Strausstown success spurring her on, she

■ **ABOVE: Shania Twain was one of Taylor's earliest influences.**

11

made her first visit to the country capital with her parents to leave demos at record companies on Music Row. The trip ended in rejection and disappointment, but she learned a valuable lesson; "That's when I realized that I needed to be more. I needed to know how to do something more than just sing a song."

Taylor began performing "The Star Spangled Banner" at sporting events and was once high-fived by rapper Jay-Z at a Philadelphia 76ers NBA game. A year after the Nashville visit, she started to play guitar when family friend Ronnie Kramer came to fix the computer and taught her three chords. Taylor being Taylor, she was soon writing songs, the first being "Lucky You."

In April 2004, and with the wholehearted backing of her parents, she began working with Dan Dymtrow, a talent representative based in New York who had numbered Britney Spears among his clients. Dymtrow helped her place a song she'd written, "The Outside," on a Maybelline Cosmetics compilation CD called "Chicks With Attitude," an annual event to help young female artists get started. Dymtrow also brokered meetings with major record companies.

After she performed at a record-company showcase, RCA offered the 13-year-old an artist development deal. According to Taylor, the company agreed to, "Sponsor and pay for your demos that you do over this next year, and we're going to see how you grow as an artist. And then in a year, we're going to decide whether we want you or whether we want to develop you for more time, or whether we want to drop you."

The deal involved many trips to Nashville, and this constant to-ing and fro-ing provoked a major family decision. When Taylor was 14, her father transferred to the Merrill Lynch office in the city and moved the family to Hendersonville, a prosperous suburb. This, as Taylor acknowledged, "was an incredible sacrifice for my parents to make and I've never forgotten it." For her freshman and sophomore years, Taylor attended

Hendersonville High School.

RCA suggested she write with veteran songsmiths like Troy Verges, Brett Beavers, Brett James, Mac McAnally, and the Warren Brothers. These collaborations were short-lived, but she would form a lasting relationship with another writer, Liz Rose. Nearly 30 years Taylor's senior, Rose had come to songwriting relatively late in life. Nevertheless, their after-school songwriting sessions were fruitful. "I love writing with Liz," said Taylor, who explained that she was the instigator of the songs' ideas. "When we write, I usually come in with a melody and some lyric content, and then we'll work on creating the rest of the song. She's a really good song editor."

A parting of the ways with RCA came at the end of the development deal after a disagreement as to Taylor's future direction. The company wanted her to wait until she was 18 and then record an album of other people's songs, while Taylor wanted to record her own material immediately. Manager Dymtrow was let go because Taylor felt that she wasn't making enough progress. In the meantime, she signed a publishing deal with Sony/ATV Tree. Arthur Buenahora, the Sony executive who signed Swift said, "The songs were great, but it was her, really. She was a star. She lit up the room." He added, "I liked her attitude. She was very easy to root for." Soon Taylor would find a record company that felt the same way and her career would truly be under way.

■ **ABOVE: Taylor pictured with Liz Rose – one of her co-writers.**

Teenage Tales

When Taylor performed at an industry showcase at Nashville's Bluebird Café in 2005, she was seen by Scott Borchetta, a DreamWorks executive who was on the verge of launching a label. As a result, Taylor became the first signing to his own Big Machine Records. For his part, Scott later revealed he had already heard her demo tape before seeing her at the Bluebird Café. "From our very first meeting, I've thought that Taylor was an extraordinary talent," he said in 2009. His faith in her was unshakeable. "That was four years ago, when she was just 14. I've never thought of her as a little girl. She's always been just an incredible young artist to me. I've had very aggressive plans for Taylor since day one."

As a self-confessed "kid of the internet," Taylor already had, in Borchetta's words "a really cool website." He was immediately able to use this and her page on the social networking site MySpace to market her and start to build up a fanbase. The buzz around Taylor began to intensify as she was featured on the cable channel Great American Country in a series of short features. "Not everyone in the industry would have taken a chance on a young female artist like Taylor. I was not getting calls from country radio stations saying, 'Do you have any teenage female singers?' But I felt there was opportunity in country music for talented young women," says Borchetta.

Taylor's father was impressed enough to buy a three per cent interest in the new record label as Taylor began recording her debut album. Most of the songs had been written during her freshman year at high school, mainly in collaboration with Liz

15

■ **ABOVE:** Scott Borchetta signed Taylor to his label, Big Machine Records, in 2005.

■ **ABOVE: Tim McGraw was the inspiration for her debut single.**

Rose, but Taylor's schooling had not suffered – as was proved when she achieved a perfect 4.0 grade. Later, she transferred to the Aaron Academy, which offered home tutoring that suited her professional commitments, and was awarded her high-school diploma in 2008.

The debut album went through several changes in producer. Taylor had previously worked on demos with Nathan Chapman, who she described as working "in a little shed behind this publishing company I was at... I'd always go in there and play him some new songs, and the next week he would have this awesome track, on which he played every instrument, and it sounded like a record. We did this for a period of a year to two years before I got my record deal."

When it came to making the album proper, various big-name producers were tried out but, as Taylor explains, "it didn't sound the way that it did with Nathan. He had never made an album before. He had just recorded demos. But the right chemistry hit. Finally my record-label president said, 'OK, try some sides with Nathan.'" Chapman went on to produce all but one of the tracks on Taylor's self-titled debut; this turned out to be a "diary from my early teens" comprised of songs written "in real time" as the events they described were actually happening.

Of debut single "Tim McGraw," she said, "I got the idea in math class. I was just sitting there, and I started humming this melody. I kind of related it to this situation I was in. I was dating a guy who was about to go off to college. I

knew we were going to break up. So I started thinking about all the things that I knew would remind him of me. Surprisingly, the first thing that came to mind was that my favorite country artist is Tim McGraw."

"The Outside" was written when Taylor was 12. "I was going through a really tough time in school and facing a lot of rejection among my peers," she explains. "I found that I was alone a lot of the time, kind of on the outside looking into their discussions and the things they were saying to each other. They really didn't talk to me. In the process of coming to that realization, I started developing this really keen sense of observation – of how to watch people and see what they did. From that sense, I was able to write songs about

relationships when I was 13 but not in relationships."

As for "Should've Said No"... "Basically, it's about a guy who cheated on me and shouldn't have because I write songs." The song was a late addition to the album, recorded just two days before mastering was scheduled.

'Picture To Burn" is a portrait of a girl who has broken up with her boyfriend. Taylor describes it as about "just being mad" and that it is "completely, brutally honest," but also concedes that she made it humorous too. "Our Song" was composed for a specific purpose. "I wrote it about this guy I was dating, and how we didn't have a song. So I went ahead and wrote us one." Taylor sang it at her freshman year talent show and originally had no intention of putting it on the album.

In contrast to the teen-romance theme of many of the songs, "Mary's Song (Oh My My My)" was about the long-lasting marriage of the Swifts' next-door neighbors. Meanwhile, "Tied Together With A Smile" was inspired by a friend who suffered from the eating disorder bulimia.

Scott Borchetta identified "Tim McGraw" as the lead single as soon as Taylor played it for him on ukulele during an early recording session. Although many in the industry said that he should have plumped for a more conventional debut for his new artist, the decision was vindicated when the single reached Number 40 on the pop chart on release in June and went on to sell in excess of a million copies in the United States. It was also warmly received by the critics for its blend of country and pop.

Taylor was closely involved when it came to packaging the product. She designed some of

the graphics and arranged for capitalization of certain letters so that they spelled out messages, something that would become a well-loved and anticipated feature of all her albums.

The 11-track CD was released on October 24, 2006, selling 40,000 copies in its first week and debuting at Number 19 on the *Billboard* chart. The promotional schedule was rigorous. "Radio tours for most artists last six weeks," she said. "Mine lasted six *months*. That's because I wanted it to. I wanted to meet every single one of the people that was helping me out."

"Taylor Swift" certainly impressed the critics. Its creator was described as "one of the most talented, young performers on the country charts today" and was praised for "a fabulous job of blending modern country with the traditional." Another review of the album referred to her "honesty, intelligence, and idealism with which listeners of any age will be able to connect."

In addition to the radio tour, she opened for future label-mates Rascal Flatts on the final dates of their Me And My Gang tour in October and November 2006. She received just two days' advance warning, as opening act Eric Church had been let go for "playing too long." She took to the stage, backed only by a guitarist and fiddle player, and took care to play only the time allotted. The following year, she was to be support act for such established acts as George Strait, Kenny Chesney, and Brad Paisley. Later, and very appropriately, she opened for Tim McGraw and for one of her heroines, McGraw's then-wife Faith Hill.

Taylor also played gigs in her own right and appeared at

festivals. One common factor after performances were the meet-and-greet sessions she conducted with the fans that would sometimes last for up to four hours. Taylor insisted on meeting all the well-wishers and often surprised fans with her ability to recognize them from previous encounters.

"Teardrops On My Guitar," the second single from the debut album, followed "Tim McGraw" into the *Billboard* Hot 100 and also made inroads into the charts in Canada and the UK. The country chart topper "Our Song," "Picture To Burn," and "Should've Said No" were subsequently taken from the album, helping keep interest high; all sold more than a million and "Taylor Swift" went on to be certified five times platinum in the United States, platinum in Australia and Canada, and silver in Britain. It was also nominated for a prestigious Grammy Award.

Seemingly overnight, Taylor had become a major star credited with changing the face of country music and opening it up to a new

younger audience – not bad for someone still in her teens. Her statuesque 5 foot 11 inch figure and unique fashion sense gave her an immediately recognizable image. Her folksy dress style soon led to her becoming a trendsetter, with fans quick to copy her. She was to prove as creative with clothes as she was with music, putting together unusual combinations of modern and retro styles. In 2009, she launched her own sundress collection made by LEI and sold exclusively at Wal-Mart.

She rounded out her breakthrough year of 2007 with a special EP of six Christmas songs entitled "Sounds Of The Season: The Taylor Swift Holiday Collection." Originally a limited edition on sale only in a chain of retail stores, it was released the following year on iTunes and amazon.com. Continuing the tradition of Christmas records by great American singers like Bing Crosby and Frank Sinatra, the EP was a little light relief before Taylor got down to the serious business of her second album.

■ **BELOW: Taylor reacts after being nominated for Best New Artist, as presenter Dave Grohl looks on, at the 50th Annual Grammy Awards news conference, 2007.**

Girl, Interrupted

As part of her publishing deal with Sony/ATV, Taylor had penned more than 250 songs either alone or working in collaboration mainly with Liz Rose and, occasionally, the similarly experienced Robert Ellis Orrall. Rather than place them with other artists, she kept the songs for herself and the majority of her first album consisted of this material. Her intention was to use the stockpile for her second and third albums. Her prolific approach to her craft meant that she continued to compose while touring with George Strait and Rascal Flatts.

Life on the road resulted in Taylor writing songs by herself, something reflected in the songwriting credits on her second album with seven solo compositions. As she put it, "If you're in Arkansas, who's there to write with?" She explained "I've written a lot of songs by myself lately, especially since I've been alone so much on the road. I do love writing on the road. I'll find a quiet place in some room at the venue, like the locker room."

Nevertheless, Taylor was not about to allow the touring experience to influence the

content of her songs. "My goal is to never write songs that my fans can't relate to. Like road songs. As a 16-year-old girl, I could never relate to those songs about playing a different city every night. I want to write about feelings and love and the lack of love. I ask myself, 'OK, where's the song for the 15-year-old who just had her heart broken? Got that? OK, good. Now where's the song for when she falls in love again?' I like to listen to music that's about life. That's what I think my fans like, too."

While discussing her songwriting, Taylor gave an insight into the depth of her astounding creativity. "When I write a song, I hear the full production in my head. Every banjo roll, every fiddle riff, every single nuance. I think my songs really come to life once that production is behind them."

Amid the new songs

earmarked for her sophomore album, "Fearless" was older material written when Taylor was 13. She saw no difference in approach or subject matter. "When I was 13, I was writing about the same things that I'm writing about now... of course, boys! And I've always been fascinated by the way that people treat each other and the way that they interact. Stuff like that just really, really fascinates me and always has. I love writing about relationships; relationship songs are it for me. It's my comfort zone, it's my favorite thing to write about and my first album is scattered with them."

Taylor also confided in a 2008 newspaper interview that she had not kissed a boy for two years. She explained that her songs came from a very female perspective and concerned the emotional side of relationships rather than the

physical. "Sometimes if someone plays with your emotions it is so much harder to get over, whether you've kissed that guy, whether you've held hands with that guy, whatever you've done." The lyrics were not necessarily autobiographical. "You know songwriting is all about being able to paint a story and tell a story, and sometimes that's telling a story to yourself."

Reuniting with producer Nathan Chapman, Taylor began recording sessions for her next album late in 2007. There was a crucial difference this time, as Taylor was more involved in the production process and was credited as co-producer. A surfeit of songs was laid down and the best selected for inclusion on the album, which contained 13 tracks – Taylor's lucky number.

By early 2008, recording was halfway complete. The remainder of the album was finished during

two sessions, one in March and the other during the summer. Preceded by first single "Love Story" in September, "Fearless" hit the shops on November 11, 2008. Both records were an unprecedented commercial success. Based on Shakespeare's *Romeo And Juliet* but given a happy ending by Taylor, "Love Story" was a new composition that sold in excess of 7,000,000 worldwide and for a while was the best-selling country single of all time.

Another late addition to the track listing was "Forever And Always" which Taylor wrote about the deterioration of her relationship with teen idol Joe Jonas of Jonas Brothers fame. The pair had been dating since July 2008, and when Jonas left Taylor for actress Camilla Belle in October, Taylor decided to put her feelings into a song. "Last Kiss" and "Better Than Revenge" on "Speak Now" were also reportedly about Jonas.

Real life was the inspiration behind "Hey Stephen," where Taylor confessed her secret feelings for Stephen Barker Liles of the country duo Love and Theft who had supported her at several gigs.

"Fifteen" was an earlier composition about how Taylor and her best friend Abigail Anderson both fell in love for the first time and both had their hearts broken. Anderson agreed to the song, which namechecks her, being used on "Fearless," and Taylor confessed to crying when she recorded it.

Critical reaction was again generally positive and "Fearless" rocketed to the top of the *Billboard* chart. It went on to sell 6.6 million copies in America and many more across the world. The

title track (and fifth single) was a fantasy about her ideal first date. She explained her interpretation of the title. "What the word 'fearless' means to me is not that you don't have fears. It's not that you're not afraid of anything. Being fearless to me means you're afraid of a lot of things, but you jump anyway."

After some warm-up dates in the US, Australia, and Britain, the Fearless tour kicked off in Evansville, Indiana on April 23, 2009. It would conclude 14 months later with a performance at the Gillette Stadium, Foxborough, Massachusetts. Fans snapped up the tickets with

unprecedented speed, dates at New York's iconic Madison Square Garden selling out within a minute.

The itinerary embraced Japan, Europe, Australia, and Canada. She was supported by Kellie Pickler and Gloriana, while Justin Bieber opened for her British dates. John Mayer, Katy Perry, and Faith Hill all guested on stage with Taylor. In all, the 105-date tour grossed over $63 million and was seen by more than a million people. In the middle of this, Taylor found time to open occasionally for Keith Urban on his Escape Together world tour.

The year also saw her make her acting debut in an episode of the television drama *CSI: Crime Scene Investigation*. Her portrayal of a rebellious teenager was hailed as a success. Soon afterward, she appeared as guest host on *Saturday Night Live*.

In September 2009, Taylor became unwittingly embroiled in controversy when accepting the MTV Video Music Award for Best Female Video for "You Belong With Me," the first country artist to be so honored. Rapper Kanye West interrupted her acceptance speech, grabbing the microphone from her and expressing the

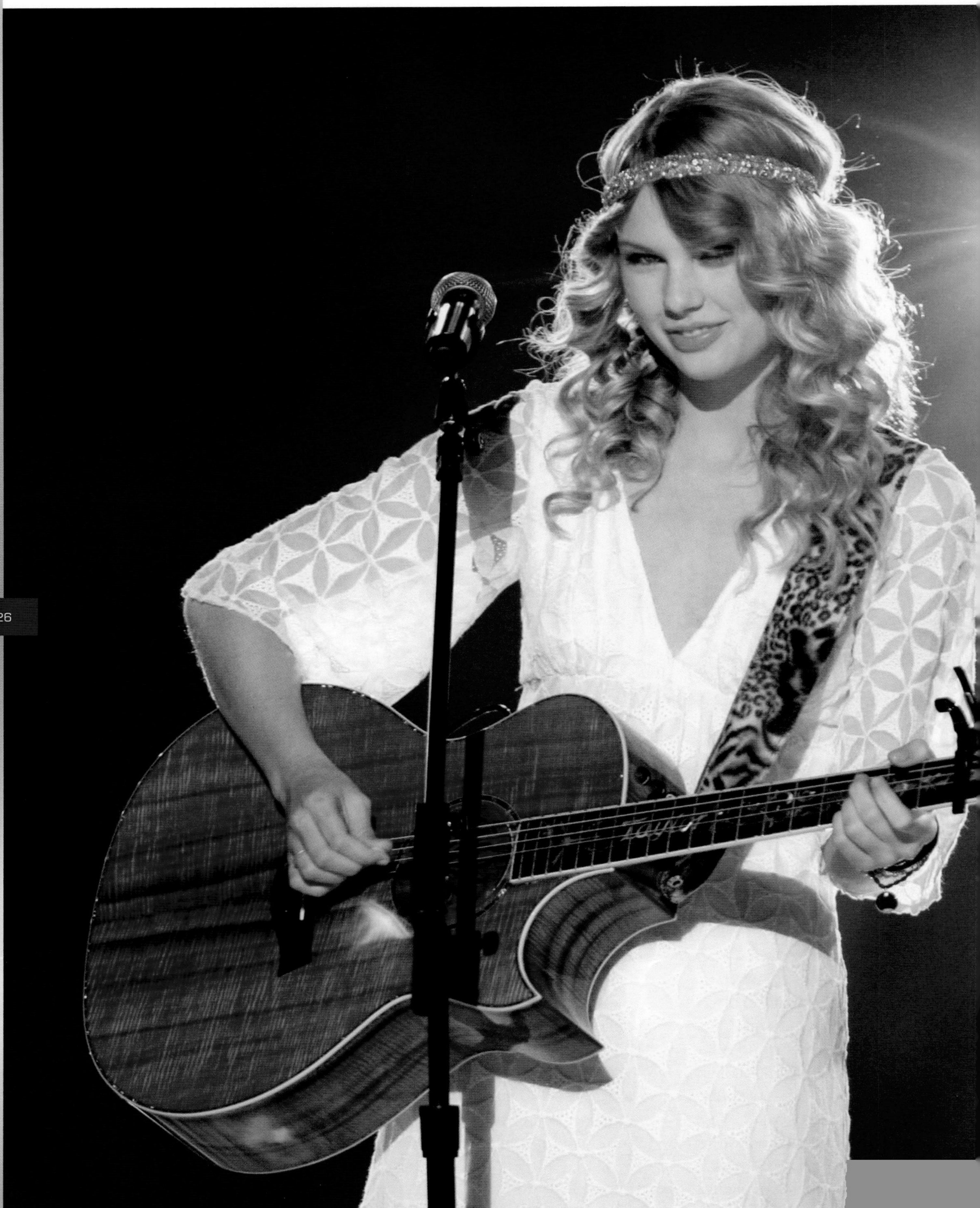

opinion that Beyoncé should have won. When booed, he flipped the crowd an obscene gesture and was subsequently ejected from proceedings.

Taylor was seen crying hysterically backstage. The incident received extensive press coverage and even President Barack Obama was said, off the record, to have referred to West as a "jackass." Kanye subsequently called her to apologize. The attention focused on Taylor, for whom most people felt great sympathy, had the effect of making her a mainstream celebrity.

2010 saw Taylor receive more awards, under happier circumstances. At the 52nd Grammy Awards, "Fearless" won Album of the Year and Best Country Album. At just 20 years of age, Taylor was the youngest person to receive the former. "Fearless" had completed a clean sweep of the corresponding title in the American Music Awards, Academy of Country Music Awards, and Country Music Association Award – the first time that this feat had been achieved, making it the most "decorated" country album of all time.

The album performed some notable feats in the *Billboard* pop chart too, remaining in the Top 10 for a full year – something only achieved by 17 other albums in chart history. In total, it spent 35 weeks, non-consecutively, at Number 1. This success was replicated in other territories. "Fearless" had catapulted Taylor Swift into a different league. But this posed a big, big question – how would the girl who preferred to write about teenage romance cope with this level of stardom?

■ ABOVE: **Kanye West takes the microphone from Taylor as she accepts the Best Female Video Award during the MTV Video Music Awards, 2009.**

27

Global Ambition

A two-year gap between albums might seem lengthy – but as Taylor explained on the eve of the release of her third album, "Speak Now," in October 2010, the creative process has been continuous. "I've been working on it for two years. Ever since we put out 'Fearless' I've been writing for this record and conceptualizing it and putting it together in my head, what I wanted it to be. I like to take a lot of time between albums to work up the next one and see what it is. We did the same thing with 'Fearless.' We put two years in between it and 'Taylor Swift' and that gives enough time for me to write everything that I live. You have got to give yourself time to live a lot of things so you can write a lot of things."

Taylor wrote all the songs herself for "Speak Now," resulting in a more personal album. "It didn't really happen on purpose," she explained, "it just sort of happened that way. I'd get my best ideas at 3am in Arkansas, and didn't have a co-writer around, and I'd just finish it. And that would happen again in New York; that would happen again in Boston; that would happen again in Nashville."

After finishing the mammoth Fearless tour, Taylor took some

time off in summer 2010, moving into her own house (in Nashville, naturally) for the first time. She continued to write songs all the while. "The thing is, I don't really talk about my personal life in interviews, but I definitely sing about it. So they're definitely very sung about on this next record."

Previewing the album, Taylor said, "I would consider the songs on this record as emotions – that's what they're about. There are some that are about infatuation and adoration and the positive, magical feelings of love. But then there are the ones that deal with when it goes wrong, which it often does. And all the different ways that it can go wrong and all the different ways it can make you feel and all the different phases of that you go through."

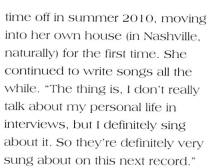

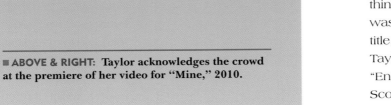

■ ABOVE & RIGHT: Taylor acknowledges the crowd at the premiere of her video for "Mine," 2010.

She described "Speak Now" as a "collection of confessions, things I wish I had said when I was in the moment." As for the title, that was significant too. Taylor's working title had been "Enchanted," but label boss Scott Borchetta felt that was inappropriate because the lyrics were not about "fairy tales and high school" any more.

Taylor came up with the new title to reflect the more mature

nature of her words and, perhaps, also as a reminder to herself to speak when in the moment – recalling the words of the minister at traditional wedding services: "Speak now or forever hold your peace." She offered a further explanation that the title "pertains to the album as a concept and as an entire theme of the record, more than I can even tell you."

She went further in explaining her creative ambitions. "This is an album, and I'm really, really in love with the idea of making an album. I don't really have much of an interest in having a few possible radio singles and then filling in the blanks with whatever you have. For me, putting out an album means that every song on that album has to be something that I thought was the best thing I've ever written when I wrote it."

The album's lead single, "Mine," was released on August 4, 2010 and was "a song that is about my tendency to run from love. It's sort of a recent tendency." She expanded on this, saying that "Every really direct example of love that I've had in front of me has ended in goodbye and has ended in breakups and things like that. So I think I've developed this pattern of sort of running away when it comes time to fall in love. This song is sort of about finding the exception to that." The single was released two weeks ahead of schedule because of an online leak.

Announced in November 2010 and starting in Singapore in the following February 2011, the Speak Now world tour was to be even bigger and better than its predecessor. Taylor was clearly relishing the prospect. "The Fearless tour was so much fun and even more unforgettable than I ever imagined, and I can't wait to get back out and play my new music. The fans have been so amazing, and I'm thrilled to play in new cities around the world and meet even more of my fans in 2011!"

The tour turned out to be spectacular indeed. She undertook many costume changes during each show and demonstrated her musical versatility by playing several different instruments. The stage set was an elaborate Broadway-inspired creation and the performances were well rehearsed and choreographed. Taylor admitted that "it's a very theatrical show, and it really reminds me a lot of my favorite musical theater productions in its scenery, costumes, and production."

Despite the scale and grandeur of the spectacle, she liked to leave some room for spontaneity.

During the North American leg of the tour, Taylor would play an acoustic cover version of a song by a local artist. For instance, when Taylor performed in Newark, New Jersey, she played Bruce Springsteen's "Dancing In The Dark." "It's been fun to be able to vary up the show so much, especially because you'll have a lot of people who will come to more than one show, and I want them to get a different experience every time," she explained. The fact this mini set was performed alone with her guitar on the smaller "B stage" at the far side of the arena only added to the effect.

Another unique aspect of the tour was Taylor's arm art. Every night she would write song lyrics (occasionally quotes from movies or famous speeches) along her left arm. She spoke about how the practice started, "One day at rehearsals I was having a rough day, and I wrote a lyric by my friend Selena Gomez on my arm: 'You've got every right to a beautiful life.' It looked cool, so now I put lyrics on my arm every night. It's like a mood ring." Songs featured were as diverse as Eminem's "Lose Yourself," KT Tunstall's "Fade Like A Shadow," and "November Rain" by Guns N' Roses.

Guest appearances by well-known names also lent an element of unpredictability to the gigs. In August 2011, Taylor invited rapper Nicki Minaj to perform her single "Super Bass" at the Staples Center, Los Angeles

simply because she liked the song so much. After that, Usher and TI showed up in Atlanta, one of her role models Shawn Colvin duetted with her in Austin, and Jim Adkins of Jimmy Eat World appeared in Phoenix.

Nashville was treated to Ronnie Dunn, Tim McGraw, Kenny Chesney, and Paramore's Hayley Williams. At Madison Square Garden, New York, Selena Gomez and James Taylor shared the stage with Taylor as the North American leg of the tour closed in November. "I'm just as shocked by it as all the fans are in the audience," said the star of the show. "The fact that they would spend their evening coming out and playing for free for my fans."

The year of 2011 ended with Taylor Swift being voted *Billboard* magazine's Woman of the Year. She accepted the award in recognition of her achievements at the annual *Women In Music* event on December 2. The Speak Now tour finally concluded in 2012 with shows in Australia and New Zealand, the final gig taking place on March 18 in Auckland.

Performance, and Best Country Song for the single "Mean." At the ceremony in February 2012 "Mean" won in both categories and Taylor performed the song live at the televised event.

Reflecting at the end of 2011 on the success of her music, Taylor was typically modest. "Growing up in this position, making music, writing songs, and having everyone hear what I'm going through since I was about 16 years old – I wouldn't have had it any other way."

She remained very much her own woman, in control of her career and not about to let others dictate her schedule. "I know exactly where I'm going to be next year at this time. That's because I'm sitting there in those management meetings every single week and scheduling everything and approving things, or not approving things, based on what I feel is right for my career at this point." This was a female who knew just where she was going.

Taylor's first stadium tour had visited four continents and grossed more than $100 million.

In October 2011, Taylor launched her own brand of perfume, Wonderstruck, comparing the effect of perfume to that of music. "I think that fragrance has a lot to do with shaping people's memories in the way that music does. If you hear a song for the first time when you are in love with someone and then you break up and you hear the song again a couple years later, it's gonna make you think right back to that moment when you first heard the song,"

In November 2011, "Speak Now" was nominated for no fewer than three Grammy Awards – Best Country Album and Best Country Solo

Acting Her Age

■ ABOVE: Taylor performs songs from her album "Red" on stage at a shopping center after switching on the Christmas lights, London.

In March 2012, Taylor contributed two songs to post-apocalyptic movie *The Hunger Games*. "Safe And Sound" was co-written with Joy Williams and Paul White, the singer-songwriter duo known as the Civil Wars. The second song, "Eyes Open," did not feature in the movie but was the lead single from the soundtrack album *The Hunger Games: Songs From District 12 And Beyond*.

April saw Taylor win the coveted Country Music Association Award for Entertainer of the Year for the second time. Back in 2011 she had been only the sixth woman and the youngest artist ever to receive the accolade.

The summer of 2012 saw a new man enter Taylor's life, 18-year-old Conor Kennedy, the son of Robert F. Kennedy, Jr. and one of the youngest members of the prominent Irish-American family. But they were to be together for just three short months.

Her eagerly anticipated fourth album "Red" represented something of a departure for Taylor both in terms of songwriting and production. After writing the whole of "Speak Now" solo, she decided that the time was right to collaborate again, although nine of the songs were composed by her alone.

Swift told MTV News "This album is interesting because each song stands on its own. It's this patchwork quilt of different sounds and different emotions... Each song is its own approach to what that particular emotion sounds like, and it's a really, really different record from anything

else I've ever done before."

Taylor previewed "Red" in a live webcast on YouTube on August 13, 2012. Over 72,500 people tuned in to see her looking stunning in red dress and matching lipstick. She chatted with fans in real time after performing "We Are Never Ever Getting Back Together." She began the discussion by talking about the significance of the album title, which was chosen not only for its simplicity but also to reflect the feelings she had experienced over the past two years.

"All the different emotions that are written about on this album are all pretty much about the kind of tumultuous, crazy, insane, intense, semi-toxic relationships that I've experienced in the last two years. All those emotions – spanning from intense love, intense frustration, jealousy, confusion, all of that – in my mind, all those emotions are red. You know, there's nothing in-between. There's nothing beige about any of those feelings."

For the song chosen as the lead-off single, "We Are Never Ever Getting Back Together," she called on the services of dance-pop producer/songwriters Max Martin and Shellback, who had worked with Maroon 5, Pink, and Kelly Clarkson. This resulted in a poppier sound than previously, so an alternate version was released to country radio. The song itself was inspired by rumors that she was getting back together with an old flame, a notion she firmly rebuffs in the lyrics.

She explained how the song was created. "I brought in this chorus to Max Martin and Shellback and just kind of played it for them, and it was just piano/vocal, and I was like, 'At the end of the chorus, I want it to just explode,' and it ended up having a little bit of a flare to it that is reminiscent of dubstep," Swift said. "It's very subtle, but I'm really excited because it actually sounds like the intensity of that emotion that I wrote about."

The Martin/Shellback team also co-wrote and produced two other songs on "Red," "22" and "I Knew You Were Trouble," the latter being the third of four promotional singles circulated in the weeks leading up to the release of the album on iTunes after being previewed on *Good Morning America*. The song was something of a departure for Taylor, bringing elements of pop and electronic rock into her sound.

In addition to the familiar pairing of Taylor and Nathan Chapman, "Red" featured a host of guest contributors. Singer-songwriter Dan Wilson, erstwhile leader of the band Semisonic, produced and co-wrote "Treacherous," while well-traveled Irish producer Jacknife Lee did the honors on "The Last Time," which featured Irish band Snow Patrol's Gary Lightbody on vocals.

A second duet, with English musician Ed Sheeran on the jointly written "Everything Has Changed," was produced by Butch Walker, a man better known for his hard-rock productions. (Sheeran would reprise the song nightly with Taylor on her 2013 tour promoting "Red" when he was announced as her opening act.) Another unexpected occupant of the producer's chair for "Holy Ground" and "The Lucky One" was Jeff Bhasker, noted for his work with Taylor's one-time nemesis Kanye West.

The now-traditional cryptic sleeve notes were discussed in

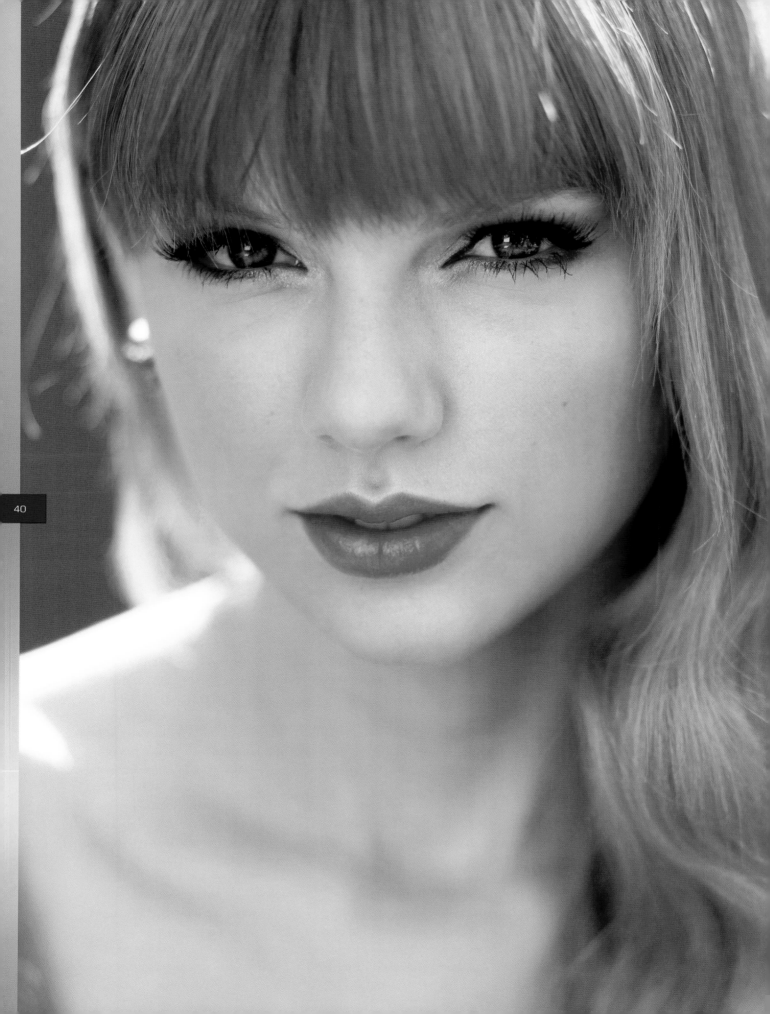

the webcast. Taylor said that, "It's pretty difficult to come up with them because I know that you guys are going to figure it out." At the same time she was grateful for the fans' close scrutiny of her words. "I'm really excited about the fact that you guys care about lyrics. Hiding little codes in lyrics is kind of a way of encouraging that."

Among the exclusives Taylor gave that day was the news that the new album would feature 16 tracks. As with previous albums, this was whittled down from a much bigger collection of songs, 35 to 40 in this case. She told the fans at the webcast that singing was her first love, despite her second career in acting. "I would love to do a movie that I was so obsessed with that I couldn't think of anything other than shooting that movie. I love music, and I love touring, and I love seeing you guys all the time, and so it's really hard to take time away from doing that. I don't like to."

Variety has since reported that she has been signed up to play Joni Mitchell in the movie adaptation of Sheila Weller's book *Girls Like Us*. The bio-pic, concerning singers Mitchell, Carly Simon, and Carole King, sounds like the ideal project for Taylor, combining as it does music with acting.

"We Are Never Ever Getting Back Together" was released in August 2012, quickly becoming Taylor's first Number 1 on the *Billboard* Hot 100 when it completed a dizzying jump from 72 to the top within the space of a week. This was mainly due to digital sales and Taylor claimed a new record when the track reached Number 1 in the iTunes chart within 36 minutes of going on sale.

■ **ABOVE:** Taylor is interviewed at the launch of her new album "Red."
■ **BELOW:** Ed Sheeran.

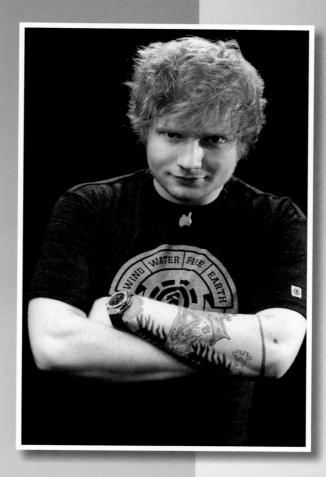

Released on October 22, 2012, "Red" shifted 1.2 million copies in its first week, making Taylor the first female artist to have two albums sell seven-figure quantities within seven days. She thanked her fans personally on Twitter: "How is this real life?! You are UNREAL. I love you so much. Thanks a million ;)."

Taylor graced the cover of the late-October issue of *Rolling Stone* magazine, but her interview appointment got off to a bad start when she reportedly backed into a parked car while using Google Maps on her iPhone! An appearance at the 2012 Country Music Association Awards in Nashville proved tricky, too, as she had just split from Conor Kennedy. The show's hosts Carrie

■ **ABOVE:** Taylor sings a track from the new album "Red."

Year, Female Vocalist of the Year, and Musical Event of the Year for "Safe And Sound," her *Hunger Games* movie track written with the Civil Wars. However, this year she was destined to leave the awards show empty-handed.

The year of 2012 closed in happier style when Taylor was booked to usher in the New Year in New York City's Times Square just before the stroke of midnight on December 31. She joined a long and illustrious list of celebrities who had previously performed on the *Dick Clark's New Year's Rockin' Eve* TV special, now hosted by *American Idol*'s Ryan Seacrest after iconic DJ Clark passed away.

The upward trajectory of Taylor Swift's career looks set to continue. Her attention to detail, hard work, and insistence of moving forward with each release have helped to build a fanbase that can readily identify with her and feels a genuine connection with her. She had achieved four multi-platinum albums by the age of 22. Since the Kanye West incident, Taylor has been dubbed "America's sweetheart," her sunny public image and natural charm making her unique in a cynical business.

While further acting work looks likely, music will always remain Taylor's first love. She will continue to do what she does best, recording, touring, and documenting her life in song. The future looks bright but Taylor Swift prefers not to look too far into it. "I've always hoped that I continue to write music for the rest of my life, and the clearest future I see is always my next album because I'm always obsessed with the latest song I've written, my newest idea about the newest thing for my newest album."

Underwood and Brad Paisley cracked jokes about them "Never Ever Getting Back Together" that seemed to have everyone laughing except, perhaps, their subject – certainly, the cameras failed to cut to her as they did to every other celeb for every other punchline.

Taylor was nominated in the categories of Entertainer of the

Fact File

Name: Taylor Alison Swift
Nicknames: Tay, Swifty
Date of Birth: December 13, 1989
Place of Birth: Reading, Pennsylvania, USA
Vital Statistics: 34-25-35
Height: 5 feet 11 inches
Weight: 120 to 125lbs
Shoe Size: Between 8 and 8.5 (US)
Superstitions: Paints a 13 on her right hand before she plays a show
Religion: Christian
Hair Color: Blonde
Eye Color: Blue
Star Sign: Sagittarius
Parents: Andrea and Scott Kingsley Swift
Siblings: Brother Austin
Marital Status: Single
Children: None
Favorite Foods: Cheesecake, scrambled eggs, Pop Tarts, cinnamon toast crunch cereal
Favorite Colors: White and purple
Favorite TV Shows: *CSI*, *Grey's Anatomy*, *Law & Order*
Favorite Movie: *Love Actually*
Favorite Musicians: Katy Perry, Keith Urban, Tom Petty, John Mayer, Hanson, Shania Twain, Faith Evans, the Dixie Chicks, Kenny Chesney, Garth Brooks, Def Leppard
Favorite Song: "Can't Tell Me Nothin'" by Tim McGraw
Hobbies: Playing guitar, songwriting, "driving past our ex-boyfriends' houses" with a friend, boating, watching movies
Lucky Number: 13

Friends and Lovers

Taylor Swift's rise to fame has been a rollercoaster ride, but the young star has had many people help and support her along the way – both personally and professionally. Her family, parents Andrea and Scott along with brother Austin, are the constants among the sea of hangers-on, and her parents helped mold her career from long before her breakthrough in 2006.

Andrea is now part of Taylor's management team, while Scott has always been around to lend his support. Referring to her happy family life, Swift once said of her parents: "They have always been very respectful of me so I've always been really respectful of them. My worst fear is to let them down, so that's why I don't misbehave."

Though Taylor can reel off a list of celebrity friends, like pop sensation Selena Gomez and actress Emma Stone, her best friend is someone who lives her life well away from the fame game. Swift met Abigail Anderson on their first day of their freshman year in 2005, and Taylor would later express Anderson's importance in her life in her 2009 hit "Fifteen." Though Anderson has made appearances in a handful of Swift's music videos, her relative anonymity is no doubt a grounding influence on the singer.

Taylor has co-written many of her hits with others: Liz Rose was a partner in rhyme, while others she has collaborated with include Robert Ellis Orrall, Angelo Petraglia, and English musician Ed Sheeran.

Being thrust into the limelight at such a young age, Swift has had to live out her teen years firmly in the spotlight. As such, the man on her arm has always been the subject of intense speculation by fans and the media alike. It's no doubt a tough thing to endure at times, with everyone seeking to know everything about your

■ ABOVE: **Taylor pictured with Selena Gomez.**

■ **RIGHT INSET:** Jake Gyllenhaal was said to be the inspiration behind the song "We Are Never Ever Getting Back Together.".

relationships, but Taylor gives one and all an insight into her personal life through her music.

She freely admits her relationships provided much valuable songwriting material. "It's mind-blowing how some guys have just handed me inspiration for some of these songs on a plate. Some have said, 'Please don't write about me,' but only when we're in the process of breaking up."

She was unrepentant about the process. "If a man dates me, he's kind of signing a waiver saying he's cool with me writing songs about him. I write songs about my life: it's not something I've kept secret."

Arguably no album is more revealing than fourth album, "Red." The record provides glimpses into her past relationships – both subtle and not so subtle – an example of the latter being lead single "We Are Never Ever Getting Back Together." If the title wasn't self-explanatory, lyrics like "I'm really gonna miss you picking fights" and "I say I hate you, we break up, you call me, I love you" show the writer's frustrations at the tempestuous nature of the relationship.

Perhaps surprising though is the apparent revelation that the ex in question is actor Jake Gyllenhaal. When told on a US chat show that fans suspected the track to be about the *Donnie Darko* and *Source Code* actor, Swift replied: "I didn't know that that was a thing that people had figured out."

The pair began dating in October 2010 and immediately

raised eyebrows due to the nine-year age gap. Then 30-year-old Jake was already a Hollywood mainstay while Swift was still the bright young country star. However, the relationship lasted just two months, with the pair splitting in December. Reports claimed that the romance "fizzled out," though Taylor's track, released two years later, suggests that the fling – and subsequent break-up – was anything but boring.

While Gyllenhaal was one of the more high-profile of Taylor's personal relationships, her first was with fellow teen star and one third of pop-rock trio the Jonas Brothers, Joe Jonas, when the pair were fresh-faced 19-year-olds in July 2008. The puppy love was short-lived, though, and the pair split just three months later in October after Jonas broke his beau's heart on the phone. Never one to bury her feelings for an ex, Taylor penned "Forever And Always" on second album "Fearless" about Jonas, featuring stinging lines that suggested her honesty had made him "hide like a scared little boy."

Personal songs about boys and exes are Taylor's calling card, but what happens when her personal and professional worlds collide? It happened toward the end of 2009 when Taylor hooked up with singer-songwriter John Mayer. Swift appeared on a Mayer track called "Half Of My Heart" which hit the US Top 30 upon release a year later. She spoke of her admiration of Mayer as they began collaborating, admitting she was "starstruck" and calling the notably hard-to-tie-down singer "amazing and sweet." It was perhaps no surprise when the pair started dating – but equally predictably it wasn't to

last the distance; the pair went their separate ways in early 2010.

The result of their fling and seemingly messy split was said to be "Dear John" from Taylor's third album, "Speak Now." Though the title may fit like a glove, leading Mayer to tell *Rolling Stone* magazine that he was "humiliated" by the song, Swift later said that the singer was "presumptuous" for assuming he was its subject. But with lyrics suggesting his past girlfriends had "tired, lifeless eyes 'cause you've burnt them out," who can blame Mayer for not wanting to be associated with it?

Taylor's most high-profile relationship to date was with

another Taylor – Lautner, that is. The pair met on the set of *Valentine's Day* in October 2009 and Swift immediately hit it off with the Hollywood actor. It quickly looked like the pair had more in common than just their names, and when they were spotted on a date, with Swift's mom in tow, it appeared as if they could be for keeps. Instead, they didn't even see out the year, amicably parting with several reports whispering that the teen *Twilight* star liked Swift more than she liked him.

After dating a series of men who were also in show business, Taylor had seemingly discovered that her boyfriends seemed

unable to handle her being more successful than them. "I've found that men I've dated who are in the same business can be really competitive. I've found a great group of girlfriends in the same business who aren't competitive, but a few times guys have started comparing careers and it has been... challenging.

"The last thing I think about when I fall for someone is what they do for a living as I like to get to know that person, but sometimes guys start acting weirdly toward me, especially if I get good news and they get bad... It's usually downhill from there."

Summer 2012 saw her close

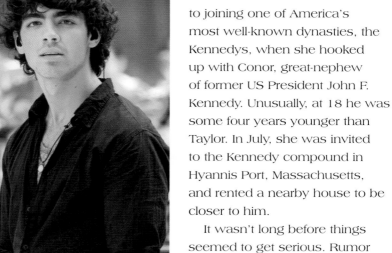

■ **ABOVE:** Joe Jonas, one of the more high-profile boyfriends Taylor has had since becoming famous.

to joining one of America's most well-known dynasties, the Kennedys, when she hooked up with Conor, great-nephew of former US President John F. Kennedy. Unusually, at 18 he was some four years younger than Taylor. In July, she was invited to the Kennedy compound in Hyannis Port, Massachusetts, and rented a nearby house to be closer to him.

It wasn't long before things seemed to get serious. Rumor had it that Taylor was about to buy a $4.9 million mansion just across the street – but ironically reports claimed that distance was to blame for their break-up in October 2012 as Swift began promoting new album "Red." Others claimed the singer had taken up with Conor's cousin, Patrick Schwarzenegger, but all parties denied this.

Taylor's romances tend to follow the same pattern: brief but intense, and more often than not creating ample songwriting material. She told *Cosmopolitan* magazine that, in her search for Mr Right, she is not prepared to waste time: "I've learned when to get out. I've never wasted too much time with the wrong person and that's one thing I'm proud of."

As for the future, Swift says she is looking for "that unexplainable spark," adding, "It's only happened a few times in my life." Given her tender age, though, the betting is that there are many more romantic twists and turns to come in the future. Until then, Swift has a support structure of family and friends that can only continue to take both her and her career to greater heights.

■ **LEFT: John Mayer performs on stage with Taylor.**

Quotes

"I'm inspired by all kinds of different sounds, and I don't think I'd ever be someone who would say, 'I will never make a song that sounds a certain way, I will never branch outside of genres,' because I think genres are sort of unnecessary walls."

"I think in terms of, in general, red is just a bold, brave color. I love red lipstick. I love red dresses. I love red shoes. I love a red stage... Red is the theme of the moment."

"I write as life happens to me, and I'm writing so much lately. It's been crazy."

"I know general things about love. How to treat people well, what you deserve, and when to walk away. Other than that, love is a complete mystery – and that's why I like to write about it."

"The only way that I can feel better about myself – pull myself out of that awful pain of losing someone – is writing songs about it to get some sort of clarity."

"The way I look at love is you have to follow it, and fall hard if you fall hard. You have to forget about what everyone else thinks."

"Everybody has that point in their life where you hit a crossroads and you've had a bunch of bad days and there's different ways you can deal with it. The way I dealt with it was I just turned completely to music."

"Most of us start to hesitate, for fear of saying the wrong thing at the wrong time. But lately what I've begun to fear more than that is letting the moment pass without saying anything."

"I've found that growing up can mean a lot of things. For me, it doesn't mean I should become somebody completely new and stop loving the things I used to love. It means I've just added more things to my list."

"I've always been a hugger. If we all hugged more, the world would be a better place."

"I love every single person who has wanted my autograph, because for the life of me I never really thought it would mean something to someone for me to write my name down."

"I've realized that before every big problem you create for yourself, before every huge mess you have to clean up, there was a crucial moment where you could've just said no."

"I think there's something so attractive about mystery. There's something so attractive about the chase. And the bad guy... bad boys know how to keep the chase going throughout an entire relationship."

"I could get drunk and run around Nashville naked. But I won't because I want to set a good example for my fans. I think they deserve to have a role model."

"My mom and I have always been really close. She's always been the friend that was always there."

"All of my favorite people – people I really trust – none of them were cool in their younger years."

Discography

Singles

"Tim McGraw"
Released: 2006
Highest US country chart position:
Number 6
Highest US pop chart position:
Number 40

"Teardrops On My Guitar"
Released: 2007
Highest US country chart position:
Number 2
Highest US pop chart position:
Number 13

"Our Song"
Released: 2007
Highest US country chart position:
Number 1
Highest US pop chart position:
Number 16

"Picture To Burn"
Released: 2008
Highest US country chart position:
Number 3
Highest US pop chart position:
Number 28

"Should've Said No"
Released: 2008
Highest US country chart position:
Number 1
Highest US pop chart position:
Number 33

"Change"
Released: 2008
Highest US country chart position:
Number 57
Highest US pop chart position:
Number 10

"Love Story"
Released: 2008

Highest US country chart position:
Number 1
Highest US pop chart position:
Number 4

"White Horse"
Released: 2008
Highest US country chart position:
Number 2
Highest US pop chart position:
Number 13

"Crazier"
Released: 2009
Highest US country chart position:
n/a
Highest US pop chart position:
Number 17

"You Belong With Me"
Released: 2009
Highest US country chart position:
Number 1 (eight weeks)
Highest US pop chart position:
Number 2

"Fifteen"
Released: 2009
Highest US country chart position:
Number 7
Highest US pop chart position:
Number 23

"Fearless"
Released: 2010
Highest US country chart position:
Number 10
Highest US pop chart position:
Number 9

"Today Was A Fairytale"
Released: 2010
Highest US country chart position:
Number 41
Highest US pop chart position:
Number 2

"Mine"
Released: 2010
Highest US country chart position:
Number 2
Highest US pop chart position:
Number 3

"Back to December"
Released: 2010
Highest US country chart position:
Number 3
Highest US pop chart position:
Number 6

"Mean"
Released: 2011
Highest US country chart position:
Number 2
Highest US pop chart position:
Number 11

"The Story of Us"
Released: 2011
Highest US country chart position:
n/a
Highest US pop chart position:
Number 41

Highest US pop chart position:
Number 7

Guest Appearances

"Better Than One"
(Boys Like Girls featuring
Taylor Swift)
Released: 2009
Highest US pop chart position:
Number 18

"Half Of My Heart"
(John Mayer featuring
Taylor Swift)
Released: 2010
Highest US pop chart position:
Number 25

"Both Of Us"
(BoB featuring Taylor Swift)
Released: 2012
Highest US pop chart position:
Number 18

Albums

Title: **Taylor Swift**
Released: October 24, 2006
Highest US country chart position:
Number 1
Highest US pop chart position:
Number 5
Sales certification: 5x Platinum

"Tim McGraw"
"Picture To Burn"
"Teardrops On My Guitar"
"A Place in This World"
"Cold as You"
"The Outside"
"Tied Together With A Smile"
"Stay Beautiful"
"Should've Said No"
"Mary's Song (Oh My My My)"
"Our Song"
"I'm Only Me When I'm With You"
(deluxe edition)
"Invisible" (deluxe edition)
"A Perfectly Good Heart"

"Sparks Fly"
Released: 2011
Highest US country chart position:
Number 1
Highest US pop chart position:
Number 17

"Ours"
Released: 2011
Highest US country chart position:
Number 1
Highest US pop chart position:
Number 13

"Safe And Sound"
Released: 2011
Highest US country chart position:
n/a
Highest US pop chart position:
Number 30

"Long Live"
(featuring Paula Fernandes)
Released: 2012
Highest US country chart position:
n/a
Highest US pop chart position: 85

"Eyes Open"
Released: 2012
Highest US country chart position:
Number 50
Highest US pop chart position:
Number 19

"We Are Never
Ever Getting
Back Together"
Released: 2012
Highest US country chart position:
Number 1
Highest US pop chart position:
Number 1

"Ronan"
Released: 2012
Highest US country chart position:
Number 34
Highest US pop chart position:
Number 16

"Begin Again"
Released: 2012
Highest US country chart position:
Number 10

(deluxe edition)
"Taylor Swift's 1st Phone Call with Tim McGraw" (deluxe edition)

Title: **Sounds Of the Season: The Taylor Swift Holiday Collection**
Released: October 14, 2007
Highest US country chart position: Number 14
Highest US pop chart position: Number 20
Sales certification: Gold

"Last Christmas"
"Christmases When You Were Mine"
"Santa Baby"
"Silent Night"
"Christmas Must Be Something More"
"White Christmas"

Title: **Beautiful Eyes** (EP)
Released: July 15, 2008
Highest US country chart position: Number 1
Highest US pop chart position: Number 9
Sales certification: n/a

"Beautiful Eyes"
"Should've Said No" (alternate version)
"Teardrops On My Guitar" (acoustic version)
"Picture To Burn" (radio edit)
"I'm Only Me When I'm With You"
"I Heart ?"

Title: **Fearless**
Released: November 11, 2008
Highest US country chart position: Number 1
Highest US pop chart position: Number 1
Sales certification: 6x Platinum

"Fearless"
"Fifteen"
"Love Story"
"Hey Stephen"
"White Horse"
"You Belong With Me"
"Breathe" (with Colbie Caillat)
"Tell Me Why"
"You're Not Sorry"
"The Way I Loved You"
"Forever And Always"
"The Best Day"
"Change"

Title: **Speak Now**
Released: October 25, 2010
Highest US country chart position: Number 1
Highest US pop chart position: Number 1
Sales certification: 4x Platinum

"Mine"
"Sparks Fly"
"Back To December"
"Speak Now"
"Dear John"
"Mean"
"The Story of Us"
"Never Grow Up"
"Enchanted"
"Better Than Revenge"
"Innocent"
"Haunted"
"Last Kiss"
"Long Live"

Title: **Speak Now: World Tour Live** (CD/DVD)
Released: November 21, 2011
Highest US country chart position: Number 2
Highest US pop chart position: Number 11
Sales certification: n/a

"Sparks Fly"
"Mine"
"The Story of Us"
"Mean"
"Ours"
"Medley: Back To December/ Apologize/You're Not Sorry"
"Better Than Revenge"
"Speak Now"
"Last Kiss"
"Drops Of Jupiter"
"Bette Davis Eyes"
"I Want You Back"
"Dear John"
"Enchanted"
"Haunted"
"Long Live"

Title: **Red**
Released: October 22, 2012
Highest US country chart position: Number 1
Highest US pop chart position: Number 1
Sales certification: Platinum (and counting)

"State Of Grace"
"Red"
"Treacherous"
"I Knew You Were Trouble"
"All Too Well"
"22"
"I Almost Do"
"We Are Never Ever Getting Back Together"
"Stay Stay Stay"
"The Last Time" (with Gary Lightbody of Snow Patrol)
"Holy Ground"
"Sad Beautiful Tragic"
"The Lucky One"
"Everything Has Changed" (with Ed Sheeran)
"Starlight"
"Begin Again"
"The Moment I Knew" (deluxe edition)
"Come Back... Be Here" (deluxe edition)
"Girl At Home" (deluxe edition)
"Treacherous" – demo (deluxe edition)
"Red" – demo (deluxe edition)
"State Of Grace" – acoustic version (deluxe edition)

Awards and
Nominations

Grammy Awards

2008
Nominated as Best New Artist

2010
Won Album of the Year ("Fearless")
Won Best Country Album ("Fearless")
Won Best Female Country Vocal Performance ("White Horse")
Won Best Country Song ("White Horse")
Nominated for Record of the Year ("You Belong With Me")
Nominated for Song of the Year ("You Belong With Me")
Nominated for Best Female Pop Vocal Performance ("You Belong With Me")
Nominated for Best Pop Collaboration With Vocals ("Breathe," with Colbie Caillat)

2012
Won Best Country Solo Performance ("Mean")
Won Best Country Song ("Mean")
Nominated for Best Country Album ("Speak Now")

Academy of Country Music Awards

2007
Nominated as Top New Female Vocalist

2008
Won Top New Female Vocalist
Nominated as Top Female Vocalist
Nominated as Album of the Year ("Taylor Swift")

2009
Nominated as Top

Female Vocalist
Nominated as Video of the Year ("Love Story")
Won Album of the Year ("Fearless")
Won Crystal Milestone Award

2010
Nominated as Top Female Vocalist
Nominated as Entertainer of the Year
Nominated as Video of the Year ("You Belong With Me")
Nominated as Song of the Year ("You Belong With Me")

2011
Won Jim Reeves International Award
Won Entertainer of the Year
Nominated as Top Female Vocalist
Nominated as Album of the Year ("Speak Now")

2012
Won Entertainer of the Year
Nominated as Top Female Vocalist
Nominated as Video of the Year ("Mean")

American Music Awards

2007
Nominated as Favorite Country Female Artist

2008
Won Favorite Country Female Artist

2009
Won Artist of the Year
Won Favorite Pop/Rock Female Artist
Won Favorite Country Female Artist

Won Favorite Adult Contemporary Artist
Won Favorite Country Album ("Fearless")
Nominated for Favorite Pop/Rock Album ("Fearless")

2010
Won Favorite Country Female Artist

2011
Won Artist of The Year
Won Favorite Country Female Artist
Won Favorite Country Album ("Speak Now")

2012
Won Favorite Country Female Artist

Country Music Association Awards

2007
Won Horizon Award

2008
Nominated as Female Vocalist of the Year

2009
Won Entertainer of the Year
Won Female Vocalist of the Year
Won International Artist Achievement Award
Won Album of the Year ("Fearless")
Won Music Video of the Year ("Love Story")

2010
Nominated as Female Vocalist of the Year

2011
Won Entertainer of the Year
Nominated as Female Vocalist of the Year

Nominated as Album of the Year ("Speak Now")
Nominated as Song of the Year ("Mean")
Nominated as Music Video of the Year ("Mean")

2012
Nominated as Entertainer of the Year
Nominated as Female Vocalist of the Year
Nominated as Musical Event of the Year ("Safe And Sound" featuring the Civil Wars)

Songwriters Hall of Fame

2010
Won Hal David Starlight Award ("Taylor Swift")

American Country Awards

2010
Nominated as Artist of the Year
Nominated as Artist of the Year: Female
Nominated as Touring Headline Package of the Year (Fearless tour 2009-10)

2011
Nominated as Artist of the Year
Nominated as Artist of the Year: Female
Nominated as Touring Headline Package of the Year
Nominated as Album of the Year ("Speak Now")
Nominated as Single of the Year: Female ("Mean")
Nominated as Music Video: Female ("Back To December")

MTV Video Music Award

2008
Nominated as Best New Artist ("Teardrops On My Guitar")

2009
Won Best Female Video ("You Belong With Me")

2010
Nominated as Best Female Video ("Fifteen")

2011
Nominated as Best Video With A Message ("Mean")

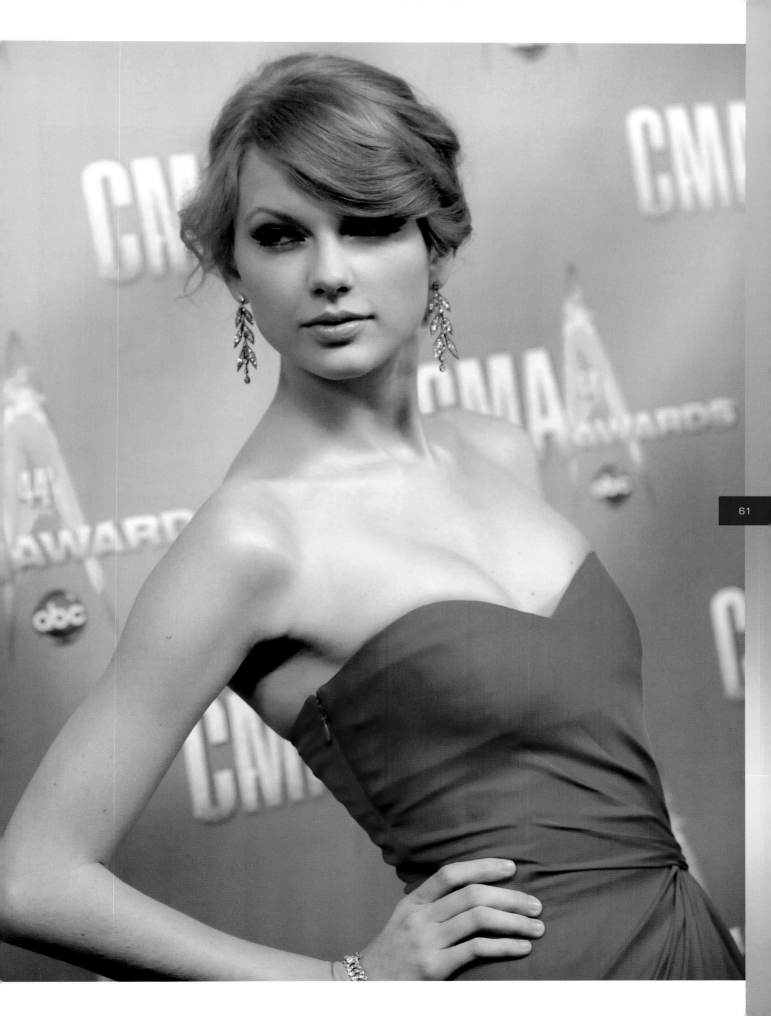

Marketing the Magic

■ **ABOVE:** A unique promotion featuring "Red" on the front of Papa John's pizza boxes.

When "Red" was released in October 2012, Taylor Swift's fans sent it to Number 1 on online retailer iTunes in an amazing 36 minutes. Those who wanted a CD to hold in their hand were able to snap it up as early as 12:01am at thousands of Wal-Mart stores. An exclusive "Zinepak" edition of the album, offered by Wal-Mart, combined a 96-page book, with photos and text, with a selection of Taylor Swift guitar picks.

By daybreak, a deluxe 22-track edition was available at Target – and if the music wasn't enough, fans could pick up a custom pair of Keds "Red" sneakers at $49.99.

Taylor's record label, Big Machine, is always looking for different ways of introducing people to her music – one of which was to offer customers of Papa John's takeaway pizza company the chance to hear and buy "Red" as part of a pizza deal that featured her image on the box.

This multi-pronged marketing campaign contributed to the album's extraordinary first-week sales of 1.21 million copies – the biggest in more than a decade. iTunes reported that first-day downloads of 262,000 set a new single-day record, a bigger figure than the majority of Number 1 albums now manage in a full week.

Big Machine opted out of releasing the album to Amazon's MP3 store in case the online retailing giant slashed the price to 99 cents as part of a promotion (as it controversially did with Lady Gaga's "Born This Way.") They also bypassed Spotify and Rhapsody, believing fans that use streaming services are less likely to buy CDs or album downloads.

Taylor was busy on her Twitter account reminding her more than 20 million followers of the upcoming release, while the day after "Red" was released she began an avalanche of TV appearances, starting with a concert in New York City's Times Square as part of her visit to ABC's *Good Morning America*. She was clearly happy to market the magic, and her fans were only too pleased to buy.

■ **BELOW:** **Taylor performs during ABC's** *Good Morning America* **at Times Square Studio in New York, 2012.**

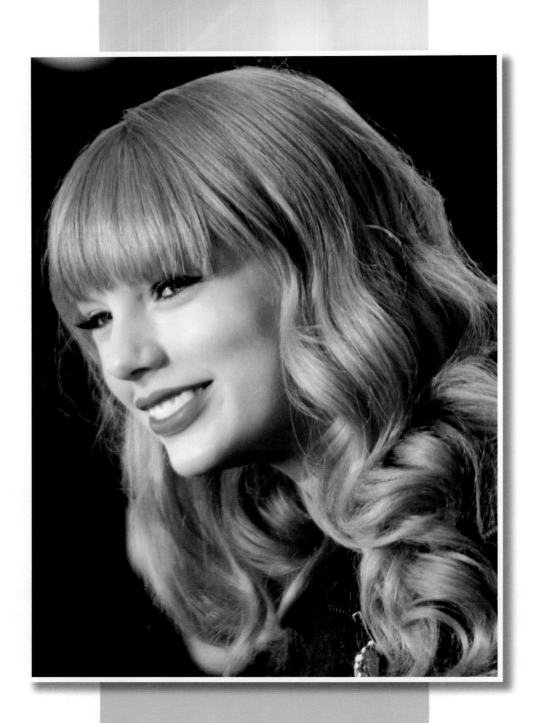